GRACE KELLY

A Life From Beginning to End

Copyright © 2017 by Hourly History.

Table of Contents

Introduction

"The idea of my life as a fairy tale is itself a fairy tale."

—Grace Kelly

Grace Kelly came into this world to join a family that was already poised for greatness. Her father John Kelley was an Olympic champion who reigned supreme over the now somewhat archaic sport of sculling. He also owned some serious financial collateral in a prominent construction firm off the eastern seaboard called the P.H. Kelly Building Company.

The company was founded in 1900 by Jack's brother Patrick and had been a source of considerable clout for the whole Kelly family. This financial clout would soon evolve into social and political influence with the eventual culmination of Jack being the Democratic Party's nominee for the mayor of Philadelphia. Jack would ultimately lose this election but little did he know that his young daughter Grace would one day become a political figure of a whole other order.

The future princess of Monaco, Grace Kelly, was born to her parents Jack and Margaret on November 12, 1929. The family, already rising in Pennsylvania's social circles, was living in the then fairly affluent Philadelphia suburb of Germantown. Here her father had built a sprawling 17-room mansion composed entirely of Kelly bricks, originating directly from the family construction business of the P.H. Kelly Building Company.

Although Grace was born into a high rising affluent family, she often felt neglected. Not in any material sense of the word, all material goods were always provided for her. But in an emotional sense, she felt a sense of deprivation. She was constantly seeking approval from her parents, but among her three other siblings, Grace felt that when it came to familial accolades, she was receiving the short end of the stick.

Unlike her siblings, who were all strong and gregarious characters just like their father, Grace was more shy and timid, preferring to withdraw inward in her pursuit of reading and the arts. In this sense she seemed most like her uncle George who was already famous in his own right as a screenwriter, winning the Pulitzer Prize for drama in 1926. It was partly due to his influence that she was able to join the East Falls Old Academy Players, a local community theatre outfit, in 1941, at the age of 12.

This would be the unofficial start of her acting career. The ambitious preteen managed to snag the lead role in a production of *Don't Feed the Animals*. Throughout the rest of junior high and high school, Grace would continue to pursue acting part-time. Grace would graduate from high school in May 1947 and embark upon the pursuit of acting fulltime. Shortly after her graduation, she is remembered to have told her mother "Now I'm really going to do what I've always wanted to do."

Chapter One

Early Modeling Career

"I avoid looking back—I prefer good memories to regrets."

—Grace Kelly

In August 1947, Kelly applied and was accepted into the prestigious performing arts conservatory in New York, the American Academy of Dramatic Arts. This meant that 18-year-old Kelly would have to leave her home in Pennsylvania and find a place to live on her own in New York City. This was a matter of some concern to Kelly's conservative Irish Catholic parents.

They had some reservations over leaving their impressionable young daughter alone to her own machinations in the big city. So much so, that they saw to it that her lodging would be one of the most strict and austere on campus, the Barbizon Hotel for Women. While she stayed in these conservative confines, Grace had to follow the house rules, a strict curfew, and most importantly of all—there could be no boys brought back to the dormitory.

Grace managed to find ways to circumvent these draconian measures, however, and was soon sneaking her love interests into the recreation room on the 13th floor of the building. One of them was Herb Miller, a young aspiring actor who Grace would sneak into Barbizon on a regular basis. And "sneak" is the operative word to describe it, because neither the authoritarian matrons who ran the place nor Grace's parents back home ever suspected a thing.

Grace was always careful to project a demure and austere facade to anyone who was interested, but deep down she had a much more wild and free spirit. A spirit that was witnessed on occasion at student get-togethers, such as an impromptu party in which after a few drinks Grace jumped onto a table and began to sensuously dance to the music.

Besides living out her wild side on occasion, during her studies at the New York Academy Grace was a serious student, and whatever her teachers asked of her she would have done. For example, when the professors of the academy let it be known that they wished to smooth out any noticeable accents among their students, Grace who had a high pitched and nasal East Coast accent jumped at the chance.

Grace Kelly began to obsessively engage in speech exercises designed to exorcise herself of her Irish-Philadelphian aural heritage. She was ultimately successful in this endeavor; when she came back to visit her family, her voice was nearly unrecognizable. It had become so prim and proper she almost sounded like she had a British accent. Something that her family found occasion to make light of, but Grace shutdown their jokes, insisting "I must talk this way—for my work."

Her family's mirth would soon give way to a newfound respect for Grace when she managed to sever her financial ties with her parents. This happened by way of a burgeoning modeling career. She was first introduced to the craft when she went with her boyfriend Herb Miller to a weekend gettogether hosted by a photographer friend of his. The man was apparently captivated by Grace, claiming that she had great bone structure and would be a perfect model for his next photo shoot.

This then led to a session with *Redbook* magazine in which Grace would end up on the cover. She was soon signed up with a high-end modeling agency, and by 1948 she was making $7.50 an hour. In the 1940s this was pretty good money, and enough to allow her to pay her own way. But not everyone was supportive of her success, and many of her classmates at the academy were jealous.

They would often deride and openly taunt her for what they believed to be snobbery on Grace's part. Like a scene right out of a movie, this tension would reach a head one day in a crowded elevator when a classmate sought to show Grace just what he thought of her by purposefully and repeatedly shoving the business end of a puppy he was carrying right into her face.

As bizarre as this treatment may seem, it was even more bizarre that no one else on the elevator seemed willing or able to get the bully to stop. Finally, a man named Don Richardson stepped into the lift. Richardson, a future bigtime director, was 27 years old at the time and was a faculty member at the acting academy.

Arriving on the scene like Grace's knight in shining armor, Richardson took Grace under his wing and put a stop to her antagonist's behavior. Richard would later recall the incident with a bit of wonder, stating, "I was amazed to realize that without knowing her at all, I felt immediately protective—I found myself treating her tenderly as a child." Richardson became Grace's protector from the moment he saw her, and that day as he walked her back to her lodgings at the Barbizon Hotel, Grace was not quite ready to leave his protective embrace.

Sensing her hesitation, Richardson asked Grace if she would like to go back to his apartment with him instead, to which she agreed. According to Richardson, after they entered his apartment, 40 minutes hadn't even passed before the two were in bed together. Grace and Richardson would then embark upon a romantic liaison that would last for several years. Never mind the fact that she was still seeing Herb Miller and other men in between, Grace would make sure that Don Richardson was a regular acquaintance.

At one point it seems, she even had desires of making Richardson something more than just a romantic fling. According to Richardson, she began to speak to him openly of marriage and their prospects of it. But these early yearnings of matrimony seem to have been cruelly crushed the weekend that she decided to bring her love interest back home to meet her parents in Pennsylvania.

Chapter Two

Parental Problems

"A person has to keep something to herself or your life is just a layout in a magazine."

—Grace Kelly

When the time came for the couple's first interaction with the family, both Don Richardson and Grace wished to make a good impression. But the chips were stacked against them, and Grace's family was determined to make the engagement as painful as possible from the very beginning. Her older brother John Jr. (known by the family as "Kell") had brought two of his college buddies for the occasion, with the express intent of being as obnoxious as possible.

And according to Richardson, they were not only incredibly boisterous and rude but also made crude anti-Semitic jokes right in front of him, with full knowledge of Richardson's Jewish roots. As you could imagine, things quickly became quite unbearable for the couple. But the total collapse of the gathering seems to have occurred when Grace's mother inquired with Richardson, "How is Grace doing at the academy?"

Thinking this was finally a point with which he could interject something positive, Richardson replied with confidence, "Oh, your daughter's going to be a very important movie star." Grace's mother, however, never wanted her daughter to go to the New York Academy in the first place, and that was the last thing that she wanted to hear. Looking at Richardson in abject disgust, she immediately informed him that Grace's stint into the world of acting was merely a "childish whim" and nothing further would come of it.

Grace meanwhile, with her love interest spurned by her family and her hopes and dreams cast away as the frivolous fantasies of a child, shrank back even further in her seat. According to Richardson, he felt sorrier for Grace than he did for himself, because of the way her family treated her. But despite this harsh treatment, Grace was still very much the obedient daughter who wished to fulfill her family's wishes.

Upon her graduation from the academy, Grace's parents ordered her to stop seeing Richardson and move out of New York to take up residence at the family vacation home in Ocean City, New Jersey. Grace dutifully did so. After abruptly moving away and cutting off contact in this fashion, it would be almost a month before Richardson heard from her again. She called him from a payphone, apparently walking almost a mile from where she stayed just to place the call.

Despite the recent distance that she had put between them, Grace would express her love to him and apologize for the hostility of her family. Richardson wouldn't hear from Grace again until she showed up in New York later that fall, just as abruptly as she had left. She had apparently been allowed to return to the city on the condition that she promised not to see Don Richardson anymore. Grace would break this vow, however, and almost immediately began seeing Richardson again.

But to Richardson's chagrin, she not only began seeing him but also other men as well. According to Richardson, it seemed that Grace was suddenly in full rebellion with her parents' wishes that she would remain a chaste young woman and was now fast becoming promiscuous. But despite her newly acquired experience with men, she wasn't quite prepared when it came to the much more sinister figures often lurking behind the scenes in the movie business.

And it was when she was trying out for a Broadway production of the famed cartoonist Al Capp's musical adaptation of his *Li'l Abner* cartoon that Grace saw the absolute worst of what powerful men in Hollywood were capable of. Richardson had dropped her off for the audition and spent the better part of a half hour at a nearby coffee shop, waiting for her to come back. As Richardson saw Grace walk through the bistro's door, he was horrified. Her hair was a mess, her lipstick smeared across her face, and her dress nearly torn off.

Breaking down in tears, Grace informed him of what had happened; she told him in no uncertain terms that somewhere along the way of discussing the prospects of her possible role in the film, Al Capp had tried to rape her. She informed her loyal confidant Richardson that she had to fight him off and run out of his office just to get away from him. Even though they were no longer a monogamous couple, Richardson was immediately filled with rage. He couldn't fathom that Grace had been treated so horribly by a man she had trusted.

So, Don Richardson, back in his full-on protective mode that he had displayed during their first meeting in the elevator, told Grace that he was going to go right down to Al Capp's office and straighten him out. It was only Grace's pleas of restraint that stayed his hand. Sadly, as is often the case in show business, Grace was unwilling to draw attention to the harassment, fearing that it would adversely affect her career. For her, it wasn't worth it, and she would much sooner forget about it and sweep the whole thing under the rug.

Putting on a brave face, Grace even attempted to make light of the horrendous episode, supposedly telling Richardson, "I'm okay—(besides)—the poor man has only one leg—leave him alone." which was a reference to the fact that Al Capp was an amputee, missing a leg. Through her bellicose sense of humor and the support of friends like Richardson, Grace was able to rebound and began auditioning for roles once again.

This time it paid off with her gaining work on the stage for the theatrical production company back in Pennsylvania called the Bucks County Playhouse. And it was probably not by much happenstance that the first role her new agency cast her in was in a play that had been written by her uncle George, called *The Torch Bearers*. Despite the murmurings among some of nepotism, it is said that Grace excelled in her performance. And with her recent accolades and renewed confidence in herself, it wasn't long before the New York intersection of 53rd and Broadway came calling.

Chapter Three

Led by the Heart

"I never say 'never,' and I never say 'always.'"

—Grace Kelly

In the fall of 1949, Grace Kelly was on the move once again and was chosen for a role in the Broadway hit *The Father*. The play was a musical tragedy about a man whose maniacal wife torments him with the thought that he isn't really the father of their child. Grace played the role of the daughter, and after the opening night of November 16, 1949, critics began to take notice, and Grace Kelly managed to steal the show, with most citing her performance as the main attraction of the whole production.

As 1949 turned into 1950, her new acclaim came just in time for the golden age of television, in which live nightly broadcasts began to hit the airwaves. In the next couple of years, Grace ended up starring in over 60 of these broadcasts, including classics such as *Lights Out,Montgomery Presents, Hallmark Hall of Fame,Studio One*, and even a brief stint on the *Ed Sullivan Show*. She was soon able to use her recognition on the small screen as a stepping stone to the big screen and gained the attention of Edith Van Cleve, a talent scout for the then movie industry giant MCA.

Van Cleve managed to get Grace a role in the upcoming movie *Fourteen Hours*. The movie ended up being a bit of a box office disappointment, not bringing in anything near what had been hoped, but it was the opening Grace Kelly needed to begin her career in film. Her appearance on the set also gained her the acquaintance of a man who was already a Hollywood veteran, Gary Cooper. She would end up starring alongside Cooper in the 1951 classic *High Noon*.

Grace had been working in Denver, Colorado as a regular cast member for the production company Elitch Gardens when on August 10, she received an official telegram from famed producer Stanley Kramer that read, "Can you report August 28th, lead opposite Gary Cooper, Tentative Title, 'High Noon.'" Grace didn't waste any time making her way to the set and threw herself full force into her role starring alongside the legendary Gary Cooper.

And that is not the only thing that she threw herself into, because—captivated by the star's charms—she soon threw herself into the arms of Gary Cooper. During the filming of the picture, she began an offscreen romance with the actor who was 28 years her senior. Grace had always gravitated toward older men, but this nearly three-decade span was pushing it, and it didn't take long for the pair's unusual relationship to hit the rumor mills.

It was actually through the tabloid gossip that had begun to circulate that the Kelly family back in Pennsylvania were first tipped off about Gary Cooper's intimate involvement with Grace. As a consequence, Grace's mother was so concerned with what was happening that she flew out to the movie set to see what was going on.

As soon as she arrived on the scene in California, Grace's mom attempted to control and monitor her daughter's activities just as she did when she lived with her in Germantown. Due to a combination of her mother's constant chaperoning and the incessant gossip that was being created, whatever had sparked the fling between Grace and Gary Cooper had been effectively snuffed out. Besides the off-scene drama, *High Noon* itself was a box office success, raking in about 18 million dollars.

Grace Kelly's next role in film would come in the epic *Mogambo* for which she auditioned in September 1952. She was quickly hired to play the part of one of the leading female protagonists, Linda Nordley. For this role, Grace would receive a steady $750 check each week. This was fairly good money for a novice actress of the 1950s. The film revolved around the love triangle of a big game hunter in Africa played by Clark Gable and his other love interest played by Ava Gardner.

With art imitating life, Grace soon fell in love with 51-year-old Clark Gable, but Gable, not wishing to be entangled with someone who was 30 years younger than him, spurned her advances for the most part. It was the first time in her young life that she had been so completely rejected by a man she admired. Grace was found to be rather heartbroken after the production of the movie came to a close. And when the group of actors landed in London and were in the process of boarding their separate flights back to the United States, Grace was even seen to break down in tears after she waved Clark Gable goodbye.

Reporters took note of this open outpouring of emotion and asked her about it later on, to which she replied in blithe denial, "If I cried, I don't remember doing so—it was probably over the fact that I had to leave all that beautiful Georgian silver behind in customs!" But truth be told, Grace had left behind a lot more than silver wear on the set of Mogambo, she had left behind her heart.

Chapter Four

Work with Hitchcock

"I've had happy moments in my life, but I don't think that happiness—being happy—is a perpetual state that anyone can be in. Life isn't that way."

—Grace Kelly

The fruits of Grace Kelly's labors in Africa came forth when *Mogambo* was released in October 1953. It was a box office hit, grossing more than four and half million dollars in the United States alone. Grace Kelly's role in the film also won her *Look Magazine*'s annual title of Best Actress for that year. It was safe to say that Grace Kelly was famous at this point and a true Hollywood Star.

As such, even more big-name directors began to come calling, and one of those directors was a man named Alfred Hitchcock. Hitchcock was in the process of developing a film adaptation of the Broadway play *Dial M for Murder*. Hitchcock felt that Grace had a rare and refined kind of beauty that would work well for the film.

Hitchcock himself described his interest in using Grace for the role in much more stark terms, when he explained, "An actress like Grace, who's a [real] lady— gives a director certain advantages. He can afford to be more colourful with a love scene played by a lady than with one played by a hussy. With a hussy such a scene can be vulgar, but if you put a lady in the same circumstances, she's exciting and glamorous."

In other words, Hitchcock believed that Grace had a real classiness about her that could be realistically displayed on screen. Despite his frank nature, Hitchcock turned out to be one of the most benevolent and benign directors Grace had ever worked with. She and Hitchcock are said to have developed quite a friendship while working together, and she considered him a great mentor in the field.

Where other directors were cold toward her and refused to answer any of her questions in regards to production, Hitchcock appeared to be an affable and readily available source of knowledge. As Grace herself would later recall, "As an actor, I learned a tremendous amount about motion picture making. He gave me a great deal of confidence in myself." Hitchcock would patiently discuss aspects of the film with her scene by scene and, after the workday was done, would even invite her over to his house to have dinner with him and his wife, Alma.

Although later women such as actress Tippi Hedren, who famously starred in Hitchcock's masterpiece *The Birds*, would report less than flattering behavior of Hitchcock, according to Grace, he was nothing but a gentleman to her at all times. She would later say of Hitchcock, "I have such affection for him and his wife that he can do no wrong." Grace and Hitchcock's professional partnership would continue over the next few years, and she would go on to star in several more films of Hitchcock's making.

The next major role Hitchcock gave her was in his epic thriller *Rear Window*, which he had begun casting for in early 1954. Kelly's co-star was the already legendary James Stewart from *It's a Wonderful Life*. The plot of this film revolved around the character of Jeff Jeffries played by Stewart, a photographer recently moribund by a broken leg, and his girlfriend Lisa Fremont played by Grace Kelly.

As the film progresses the bored character of Jeff Jeffries, cooped up in the house, gets the idea of using the telescopic lens on his camera to spy on his neighbors across the street. It was through this ill-conceived use of his camera that he witnesses several incidents that seem to indicate that a murder has taken place. In the middle of this intrigue, Grace's character of Lisa pays several visits to the home of Jeff Jeffries as the plot progresses.

All throughout the production of the film, James Stewart attests to the professionalism and quality of Grace's conduct. Thinking back on his interactions with her during the film, Stewart would later state, "A lot of things impressed me about her. She seemed to have a complete understanding of the way motion picture acting is carried out. And she was so pleasant on the set; she was completely cooperative. She was really in a class by herself as far as cooperation and friendliness are concerned." These are some pretty hefty accolades from a veteran like Stewart and stand as a testament to just how seriously Grace took her profession of acting. *Rear Window* was released to the public in August 1954 and was a complete box office smash. It was her best film to date, and it made Grace Kelly a household name.

Chapter Five

To Catch a Prince

"Hollywood amuses me. Holier than thou for the public and unholier than the devil in reality."

—Grace Kelly

Still riding high on her praise for *Rear Window*, Grace Kelly was cast in the role of Georgie Elgin in *The Country Girl*. In this film, Grace—who had previously just co-starred as a leading lady—was given for the first time top billing as a main character. Rather than just being a background piece for a leading man, in this movie her character was the main focal point of the story. For Grace, this was her big opportunity to let her talent as an actress shine.

Her husband in the film was played by Bing Crosby, a famous musician and actor in his own right. Bing, who was once again a co-star with a considerable age gap, played the part of the drunk, outdated singer that Grace Kelly's character had to contend with. Grace, seeming to have a pattern of being smitten with her older male counterparts in film, soon developed an interest in Bing, and this interest was reciprocated.

Bing's former wife, Dixie, had just recently passed away from cancer. Even though some questioned why

Bing would be involved with someone so soon after his wife's death, the fact that he was a widower put him in the clear for Grace to be able to see him off set and in public without much fear of provoking scandal. As the romantic fling progressed, Bing soon began to talk of marriage, but to his great sadness, being a wife was the one role that Grace was just not ready for, and she rejected his overtures.

The relationship soon grew cold afterward and was never rekindled. But although their chemistry off set ultimately fizzled, what they did together on the silver screen would live on, and *The Country Girl* would be another great success that actress Grace Kelly could put on her resume. She would end up winning an Academy Award for *The Country Girl* as best actress, as well as a Golden Globe.

Shortly after collecting these awards, Grace Kelly was on a plane headed for southern France to star in what would be her last movie directed by Alfred Hitchcock, *To Catch a Thief*. A friend she had become acquainted with in New York, Oleg Cassini, joined Grace on the set of the movie, and the two began to share quite a bit of quality time together. After a hard day on the set, Grace would often retire with Cassini to dine at some of the finest restaurants and cafes of France.

As they became closer and closer entwined with each other, Grace asked Oleg what his long-term plans were for the two of them, and he was quick to offer marriage. Unlike with Bing Crosby, this statement of commitment did not immediately drive Grace away. Instead, she silently agreed and began what Cassini would later refer to as a secret engagement only known to each other. It was in the midst of her romance with Cassini in southern France that Grace would first become acquainted with the trappings of what would one day be her future kingdom: Monaco.

Positioned just on France's southern Mediterranean coastline, Monaco is a modern city-state that has been ruled by a long line of monarchs from the royal house of Grimaldi. As Grace and her entourage drove by the palace of the prince of Monaco on one occasion, the magnificent gardens of the palace grounds caught her eye, causing her to remark, "Whose gardens are those?" At which one of her companions promptly replied, "Prince Grimaldi's, I hear he's a stuffy fellow."

Little did anyone know at the time, that this "stuffy fellow" would one day become Grace's husband. In the meantime, Grace and her co-stars finished up their filming of *To Catch a Thief*, and it would hit the movie theatres in August 1955. The reviews were a bit mixed, but overall the movie was considered a commercial success, and even won an Academy Award for cinematography, seeming to continue Grace's winning streak in the movie business.

But despite all of her success on the big screen, her love life was still rather tumultuous. Desperately seeking her parents' approval, she arranged to have her latest love, Oleg Cassini, take a weekend trip with her to meet her family. Much as was the case with Don Richardson all those years ago at the academy, the visit with her folks proved to be disastrous.

Oleg was immediately given the cold shoulder, and as he would later recall, "The weekend I spent [with Grace's family]—was the worst of my life. I ate razor blades for breakfast there. Nobody would talk to me except Grace's sisters. Grace's father positively refused to talk to me. He mumbled something to the effect that there was no communication possible between us ever."

Surprisingly, even though Grace was now 25 years of age and a rich and famous starlet to boot, she still relied heavily on her parents' opinions, and as a result, soon thereafter she ended her relationship with Cassini. In the meantime, Grace was looking for a new suitor, but she didn't have to look very far. In fact, she didn't have to look much further than the stomping grounds of the cast and crew of *To Catch a Thief* in southern France, in the principality of Monaco. Here she would meet—at long last—a real prince to sweep her off her feet.

Chapter Six

Dealing with Destiny

"Our life dictates a certain kind of wardrobe."

—Grace Kelly

Grace Kelly had been chosen to attend as the main attraction of the 1955 Cannes Film Festival, held annually in France. Grace landed in Paris on May 4 and prepared to board a train for the city of Cannes. Before boarding, she was intercepted by the editor of the popular French magazine *Paris Match*, Pierre Galante. Galante had apparently concocted a publicity scheme with his associates to have the famous American actress meet Europe's most famous bachelor: Prince Rainier of Monaco.

He convinced Grace to attend an arranged meeting with the prince. Grace was then officially introduced to the heir of the Kingdom of Monaco on May 6, 1955. She was almost immediately smitten by the prince as he gave her a personal tour of the palace's opulent gardens. And despite the constant flashes of paparazzi cameras, Grace suddenly felt a deep and intimate connection to the prince.

And she wasn't the only one, Rainier himself would later recall that he found himself struck by the class and refinement presented by this famous American Hollywood icon. By all accounts, if it wasn't downright love at first sight, it was pretty darn close. And ironically enough after meeting the prince and returning to the United States, in a situation that would prove to be art imitating life, Grace's next role would be as a princess in the romantic comedy *The Swan.*

The film set in 1918 revolves around the fictional Princess Alexandra who is being considered for marriage in order to help safeguard the continued propagation of an obscure European monarchy. Even while Grace played a princess on the big screen, she was contemplating becoming the real thing as Prince Rainier's courtship of her began in earnest. She received both periodic letters and phone calls from the prince.

Along with these direct forms of communication, the prince's court also sent out some tentative feelers to Kelly's parents as well. Prince Rainier's main religious consul in the Catholic church was a man by the name of Father Francis Tucker. By sheer coincidence—or perhaps divine providence—Father Tucker just so happened to know Grace Kelly's father. As fate would have it, Tucker had previously been assigned to a parish in America just outside of Philadelphia.

Besides the prince's wealth and obvious charm, he had two other factors very important to the Kelly family already in place—unlike her other suitors, he was a man of old world tradition willing to ask her parents for the permission to marry her, and as a devout Catholic, there would be no ideological schism to threaten the Kelly household. Soon Kelly's family would be just as thrilled about the match as Kelly and Prince Rainier themselves.

This then culminated in another meeting between the two when the prince embarked on an already scheduled tour of the United States in December 1955. The occasion couldn't have been better, and it was arranged for them to meet on Christmas Day. Although Grace Kelly thought the world of the prince, the idea that she might actually marry him still made her extremely anxious. So much so, that she almost canceled her plane ticket back home and called off the whole thing.

As she would later recall, "I almost didn't go home for Christmas, even though the Prince was to visit us. I made up my mind I wouldn't go. And then—I can't remember how it happened—I just went and bought a plane ticket anyway." The prince, accompanied by Father Tucker and his physician Doctor Donat, rang the Kellys' doorbell around 7 PM, and after just a few minutes of preliminary conversation, it didn't take long at all for the prince and his entourage to break the ice.

Amazingly, from the beginning Prince Rainier seemed to fit in just fine with the Kelly family, and it was quite apparent for everyone around her that Grace was quite enamored with the prince as well. Later in the evening, as her parents were nearing their bedtimes, Kelly's older sister Peggy wished to give her more time with the prince, and so invited them to her and her husband's house to further their revelry.

Here they played poker and other card games until the early morning hours. No one was sure if the prince was much of a card shark or not, but it did provide him with an excellent excuse to talk long into the small hours with his romantic interest. The group then returned to the Kelly house and everyone went off to separate rooms to sleep.

The prince and his entourage would spend the next couple of days with the Kellys, before the prince briefly accompanied Grace on December 27 as she returned to the set of her latest production, *High Society*. This film was a musical comedy and had her cast alongside co-star familiars such as Bing Crosby and Frank Sinatra. This film would ultimately prove to be Grace's last as she closed the chapter of her Hollywood life to enter a new one as the newly betrothed princess of Monaco.

Chapter Seven

The Princess of Monaco

"At times I think I actually hate Hollywood. I have many acquaintances there, but few friends."

—Grace Kelly

Once Grace Kelly and the prince of Monaco were engaged, there were only a few technical stipulations that needed to be fulfilled. The most important of which was the stipulation that the bride to be was fertile enough to bear the monarchy a future heir. Foisting a fertility test upon your fiancé is not exactly the most romantic of things to do, but it was a requirement in order for Grace to obtain the position of princess of Monaco.

In fact, Prince Rainier's previous girlfriend, French actress Gisele Pascal, had failed the same test, and this alone was enough cause to end their relationship. It would be much to the prince's embarrassment years later when he found out that Gisele had married and had children. But despite the perhaps flawed nature of the 1950s fertility tests, Grace would have to consent in order to move forward. And fortunately for her, she passed all the exams with flying colors.

With these cumbersome physical tests out of the way, the next hurdle to clear would be a financial one.

Apparently in order to marry a prince, the father of the bride was expected to pay a small dowry. As it no doubt still does today—at the time this struck almost everyone as absurd. Most Americans—the Kellys included—assumed that marrying a prince would bring money to the bride's family, not be the cause for a requested payment in advance.

Not quite understanding the long tradition of royal dowries, Grace's father quipped at the time, "I don't want any damn broken down Prince who's head of a country over there that nobody ever knew anything about, to marry my daughter!" But in reality, the dowry payment was not required because the prince was "broken down" or needed the Kelly family's money, this was simply a matter of formality and tradition.

It was Father Tucker who, after several long discussions with Mr. Kelly on the subject, finally convinced him it was for the best. And after Grace's father provided a dowry of 2 million dollars, the engagement of the pair was announced shortly thereafter, and both America and Europe exploded with excitement at the prospect of this transatlantic romance. All the newspapers and celebrity magazines heralded stories with various alterations of the headline the "Wedding of the Century," and Grace and her prince got their first taste of what it might mean to be an official couple.

The initial site of their projected marriage was to be in the Kelly home stomping grounds of Philadelphia, but after the prince's handlers objected, it was switched to Monaco. Apparently, Prince Rainier's stewards felt that the principality could not miss the wonderful opportunity that the "Wedding of the Century" would provide them when it came to the massive tourism and subsequent monetary windfall that the event would bring. With these details squared away, the newly engaged couple were scheduled to celebrate their engagement at the Waldorf-Astoria in New York on January 10, 1956.

Here the photographers, and the public at large, were allowed to have their fill of the soon to be royal couple, as they dined together and danced in the glow of camera flashes. It wasn't all unbridled, warm affection and love for the two however, and a bit of jealousy and angst managed to surface during the course of the evening. It occurred when an ex-girlfriend of the prince, a woman hailing from the high society circles of Ecuador named Graciela Levi-Castillo, came forward from the crowd on the supposed premise of congratulating the prince.

After issuing her congratulation, however, she gave the prince a passionate kiss on his cheek, right in front of Grace. The soon-to-be bride stared in disbelief at her fiancé's face, stained with red lipstick, and immediately issued the order, "Wipe that lipstick off your cheek." The prince complied and, despite his former relationship with Graciela, pretended he didn't know who she was.

But Grace knew better; she knew that Graciela was more than a random stranger and couldn't help but contemplate that perhaps this kiss and adoration of her beloved was just a taste of things to come. Grace had played around with high society on the big screen, but now she was going to have to do so in real life as well.

Chapter Eight

High Society

"The freedom of the press works in such a way that there is not much freedom from it."

—Grace Kelly

Grace Kelly returned to Hollywood to resume filming of her latest and what would be her last release, the film *High Society*. It was a little difficult for Grace to settle back into her role as actress because of the understandable spotlight that her personal life had recently received. But to Grace's horror, the glare of that light would soon get a whole lot worse when her mother suddenly decided to talk to Hollywood gossip columns about her previous romantic history.

Mrs. Kelly had apparently—without Grace's permission or knowledge—given a series of interviews to a reporter, and the contents of these discussions soon spread like wildfire across big name publications nationwide such as the *Los Angeles Herald* and the *Examiner*. Grace was completely mortified to find her mother speaking so freely about her previous relationships and so nonchalantly digging up past dalliances that she had tried so hard to keep private.

She felt completely betrayed by her mother and told those who were close to her as much, confiding in them, "I've worked so hard and now my mother's going to destroy everything overnight." But even though her mother let her down, when it came to Grace's privacy, she found an unlikely champion in MGM studios who were just as eager to protect Grace's pristine image.

And after more sultry versions of the contents of the interview were distributed in Europe, the studio made sure that the report was much more sanitized by the time it printed in the United States. Whether this bit of aid from her employer made her feel much better about the ordeal is not entirely clear, but Grace put on her brave face regardless and trudged forward with production.

The next big piece of gossip on the set of *High Society* was actually not what was circulating on the newspaper racks, but what Grace was wearing on her own finger. As she continued to play the part of the film's high society socialite Tracy Samantha Lord whose character was also engaged to be married, she decided to wear the real-life engagement ring that she had received from Prince Rainer.

The ring, set with Grimaldi family jewels, was absolutely stunning, and soon the talk of its magnificence—and just what Grace might really be getting into by marrying the prince—drowned out any untoward gossip about her past. Then in September 1956, Grace was pleasantly surprised to find her prince renting out an extravagant villa in Bel Air so that he could spend the next several weeks with her while she finished up filming for *High Society*.

As the two were spotted together with much more regularity—as if the fever of initial speculation had burst, and the reality was setting in—Hollywood began to openly speculate over whether or not Grace would indeed continue her film career after she married the prince. After being travailed upon with this question at the time, Grace allowed cold hard logic to decide for her, as she flatly informed the speculators, "My contract has four years to run. I've always been faithful to any agreement I have made."

Grace of course was referring to her MGM contract, thinking that her contractual obligations would be enough to provide evidence of her intent to continue acting. But this statement was directly contradicted by her fiancé just a few days later when Prince Rainer who had already had enough of the drama (on and off the set) of showbusiness, unequivocally stated to the press, "I don't want my wife to work. She thinks I am right—that she should end her film career."

This statement created immediate uncertainty with MGM and sparked off a bit of a legal crisis that Grace Kelly—whether she fulfilled her contract or not—wished to at least put off until after the wedding. MGM had her slated to star in their next big film *Designing Woman* later that year, but not wishing a public battle that would have them filing a lawsuit against a princess of Monaco, they ultimately backed down.

Not only that, they gave her a $65,000 bonus for her wedding, and would ultimately keep her on the payroll for her weekly wages of $1,500 for a few additional months after the wedding. But they did this with one stipulation: they wanted to have all rights to the filming of her wedding.

Grace Kelly didn't need to hire any wedding photographers for her day of matrimony—she signed a contract with MGM, allowing them to make a documentary piece out of the entire occasion, which was aptly called "The Wedding of the Century."

Grace and her prince would have their way, but would they live happily ever after?

Chapter Nine

Princess or Prisoner

"Before my marriage, I didn't think about all the obligations that were awaiting me. My experience has proved useful and I think that I have a natural propensity to feel compassion for people and their problems."

—Grace Kelly

Grace Kelly boarded an ocean liner called the USS *Constitution* and disembarked from New York's Pier 84 for her destination of Monaco on April 4, 1956. Making the eight-day journey with her were her family, friends, and eager members of the media, who—although were made to lodge far from the princess-to-be—were constantly demanding press conferences.

Meanwhile, as his bride was fending off the press, Prince Rainier was making elaborate preparations for her arrival. He wanted to make sure that everything was perfect for the wedding and its festivities since he was well aware that practically the whole world was going to be watching the event. In traditional enough fashion, the prince then took some time to cool off from these building marital pressures on April 8 by attending his bachelor's party at a private hotel in southern France.

Just a few days later, on April 12, Prince Rainier then boarded his yacht and sailed out to greet Grace arriving on the *Constitution*. As Grace's ship parked in the harbor, in truly epic fashion, the prince's yacht sped off to meet them. After the long journey Grace was overjoyed to see her prince on the deck of the yacht and waved with delight. A sturdy gangplank was then placed between the two vessels, and like a bridge from her past to her future, Grace crossed the threshold to her brand-new life with the prince.

Grace was followed on board by her parents, and the group was then ushered into the prince's cabin to catch up with each other. Grace re-emerged on the deck of the yacht as it approached the shoreline of Monaco. From her vantage point she was surprised to see well-wishers—her future subjects no less—lined up all along the harbor cheering her arrival.

The ship soon docked thereafter and champagne was called for all on board in an impromptu welcoming celebration for the Kelly family. The group then disembarked the yacht, and Grace and her family were escorted back to the prince's palace. As the cars of the entourage entered through the gates of the palace, royal guards stood to attention and an official salute and bugle call was issued at their approach.

The family was then given the official royal treatment, given lavish meals, grand tours, and having every need attended to, but this was a short respite before Grace's real challenge would begin—the wedding itself. The wedding day finally arrived on April 19, 1956, and just like Grace had dreaded, it was a paparazzi extravaganza. Besides the official film crew for the wedding with MGM, there were members of both European and American press taking photos for countless publications from Hollywood to Monaco and everywhere in between. According to Grace Kelly, the church in which she got married was so filled with photographers, some of them were literally "hanging from the rafters."

The official vows were made between Grace and the prince at Saint Nicholas Cathedral with Bishop Gilles Barthe presiding. Besides the thousands of onlookers that were spilling out of the church pews, there was a TV audience viewing the event live, estimated to be somewhere over 30 million people.

After the ceremony ran its course and prince and princess were wed, the new royal couple then embarked upon a seven-week cruise in Prince Rainier's yacht, touring destinations known and unknown all throughout the Mediterranean. Many sights were seen, and many precious moments were created during the trip, but the most important item on the itinerary was simply to steer clear of any and all news media and journalists.

Upon their return to Monaco and the palace after their honeymoon, Grace was thankful to note that all of the journalists and media hounds had packed up and gone home. But as her newlywed husband returned to his official duties as prince of the principality, she found herself isolated and virtually all alone during his working hours. Even though she was surrounded by countless servants and members of the court, her French was still considerably lacking.

She was not able to openly converse with anyone around her, making her essentially an English-speaking island in a sea of foreign discourse. In her loneliness, the highlight of her day was checking the mail and digging through it for potential correspondence from afar. To these messengers she wrote profusely as if she truly were a prisoner, trapped in a gilded cage. She also quite frequently ran up the prince's phone bill, calling back to both her contacts in Hollywood and the Eastern Seaboard of the United States.

During her husband's absence, she felt a desperate need for comfort and contact, and one month into her marriage, after finding out she was already pregnant, these feelings only intensified. Prince Rainier, feeling immensely sorry for his new bride, appointed her a lady in waiting to see to her needs, as well as teach her French in the process. Her name was Madge Tivey-Faucon, and interestingly enough, this designated helper was a friend of the prince's former lover, French actress Gisele Pascal.

It must have been somewhat painful for Gisele, who was rejected by the prince due to her perceived infertility, to have one of her best friend's play nursemaid to the woman that took her place. Madge tried her best to take care of Grace's every need, and she attempted to teach her French, just as instructed. But in regard to the latter efforts, Grace is said to have never truly learned the language sufficiently enough to engage anyone in any meaningful conversation.

This continued inadequacy with Monaco's national language of French led Grace to be uncomfortably silent during most public engagements. And as a result, Grace became so self-conscious of herself, and how she may be viewed during public interactions, that she became a kind of palace shut-in, only leaving the palace grounds when she absolutely had to. To many, it did indeed seem that Grace was fast becoming a prisoner instead of a princess.

Chapter Ten

Facing Challenges

"If anyone starts using me as scenery, I'll return to New York."

—Grace Kelly

In the first couple years of their marriage, Prince Rainier was growing more and more concerned for his wife's well-being and sought to keep her worried mind occupied by commissioning her to head a project of renovation for their 800-year-old palace. This way Grace was able to put aside some of her misgivings and throw herself completely into the work of restoration of the royal household.

Her first major step in doing so was to have all of her furnishings from the lavish New York apartment she had—until then—still been renting, shipped over to Monaco. These arrived near the end of 1956, and with them, she hoped to bring a little piece of her former life nearer to her, even as she finally cut a major lifeline from the other side of the Atlantic asunder.

In the early weeks of 1957, Grace continued her renovation activity, until the imminent arrival of her first-born child would no longer allow her to do so. The last renovation made before the impending birth was the conversion of a library into a delivery room. The room was said to have been completely draped in green silk, supposedly as an homage to one of Grace's ancestral Irish customs.

It was apparently an old Irish superstition that a child born surrounded by green will become happy and prosperous in life. It was the luck of the Irish that the royal couple was hoping for, and they were at least lucky enough for Grace to give birth to a healthy eight-pound girl, a daughter they named Caroline, on January 23, 1957. And they would get lucky once again, just five months later, when Grace became pregnant with the future heir to the throne, Prince Albert.

Grace would later recall these back-to-back pregnancies, stating, "It's hard to remember *not* being pregnant in those days." And to the joy of the entire realm, the male heir to the throne was born on March 14, 1958, finally fulfilling much of what everyone had hoped for with the union of Grace and Prince Rainier in the first place—the assured continuity of the monarchy.

The next few years with two toddlers in tow, Grace set about rearing them as best she could. She was determined from the beginning to be a hands-on mother and refused to allow any nurse or nanny to take on more of a role than herself in raising them. Schooling was conducted in the palace, in which Caroline and Albert were placed in a classroom with other fellow children from Monaco.

Grace was determined to make sure that her children had as normal of an upbringing as possible, and beyond anything else, she wished to keep them from developing the haughty attitude that plagued so many royals. In one notorious incident, Grace witnessed her son Albert crudely order a servant, "You may take my plate away!" Greatly disturbed by the child's hubris, Grace sought to take his royal highness down a notch or two, by quickly informing her son that he was fully capable of taking his plate away himself.

Grace's parenting style was rather unique, and its rarity was on full display when her daughter Caroline developed a penchant for biting her brother. No matter how many times they told the girl to stop her behavior, like a royal vampire she continued to bite. In order to teach the young Princess Caroline how wrong her actions were, Grace took matters into her own hands. She grabbed Caroline's arm and bit down on it as hard as she could to demonstrate to her just how bad such things were.

Caroline, grimacing in pain from the bite, learned her lesson, and never bothered her brother again. Such parental actions carried out today would provoke a visit by Child Protective Services and perhaps even criminal charges. But in Monaco during the early 1960s, Grace's proactive parenting was considered highly effective. And by the time her third and final child was born on February 1, 1965, parenting was one challenge that Grace, the princess of Monaco, felt more than ready to face.

Conclusion

Grace Kelly turned 40 years old on November 12, 1969, and this was a milestone that she dreaded. For her, 40 was the end of any aspirations she may have had to reignite her film career, and in her mind, it was the beginning of her slow decline, as her world renounced beauty began to fade. But her misplaced fears were far from the truth. After 40, most who knew her would contend that Grace was more beautiful than ever.

And all throughout the 1970s, she came into her own as princess, wife, and mother, like never before, managing to reign in not only her royal subjects but also the rebellious teenage years of her children. She had to especially use tender care when it came to her daughter, Caroline, who after graduating high school became a regular on the club scene and as a result a frequent target of the media.

In the end, Grace was able to help ease her children out of the worst that the turbulence of adolescence all too often provides. And by the early 1980s, her house and her life seemed to be in order once again. But on September 13, 1982, fate would sneak up on Grace Kelly and catch her completely unaware. And in a plot twist that even Hollywood couldn't write, her life story would reach a tragic conclusion.

She was driving back to the palace from the family vacation house of Roc Agel located in the Maritime Alps of southern France with her daughter Princess Stephanie when she was beset with sudden illness. Later autopsies would reveal that she had suffered a stroke. But it wasn't the stroke that killed her; it was the resulting crash off the side of the mountain that occurred when the stroke caused her to lose control of the car.

Her daughter, Princess Stephanie, would survive with fairly minor injuries. Princess Grace herself would not be so fortunate; she would ultimately succumb from the combined trauma she faced the next day, on October 14, 1982. She passed away quietly at Monaco Hospital. At the age of 52, Princess Grace of Monaco was gone, but the true grace that she showed the world will not soon be forgotten.

Made in the USA
Coppell, TX
06 January 2020